SEVEN
STEPS TO
RETIREMENT
SUCCESS

SEVEN STEPS TO RETIREMENT SUCCESS

The Only Guide You Need
to the Most Important
Transition of Your Life

By

Winter A. Troxel, RICP®

Foreword by Abe Ashton

MFC BOOKS

Published by

Monumental Financial Books

9210 Corporate Blvd.

Suite 130

Rockville, MD 20850

Manufactured in the United States of America

ISBN-13: 978-1530833436

ISBN-10: 1530833434

Cover and interior design by Sheila Hart Design, Inc.

This book is dedicated to
Brette, Corrie, and Ron.
Cheers to the group who believed in
what we were trying to accomplish
from the beginning.

Contents

SEVEN STEPS TO RETIREMENT SUCCESS

Foreword

By Abe Ashton

Dear Retiree (or Soon-to-Be Retiree),

Here's the bad news. You are facing retirement in one of the most complex and difficult financial times in modern history.

Interest rates are at an all-time low and market volatility is at an all-time high.

The number of companies offering pensions and retirement benefits is in an unprecedented decline.

Government programs, including Social Security, Medicare, and Medicaid, are dangerously close to insolvency.

There is a fierce battle raging within the financial services industry, placing you in the middle of a tug-of-war among banks, insurance companies, and Wall Street.

Countless Americans are finding themselves overwhelmed by these facts, petrified by the future that awaits them. As they vainly search for guidance, they are resorting to immobility–doing nothing at all.

But not you!

You are not hopeless or unprepared. You are part of a generation of hardworking Americans raised on the stories of parents who weathered the Depression. You listened, took these stories to heart, and saved accordingly. You would never bet the entirety of your hard-earned nest egg on Social Security alone and risk your financial well-being during your precious golden years. You've saved, invested, contributed, allocated, and accumulated. It's time to ask the big question:

Now what?

What does your transition into retirement look like, financially? How can you best move from an accumulation plan to a retirement plan? When the worst happens, how will you protect your surviving spouse and guarantee her income for life? Where can you find security while protecting yourself from low interest rates, market volatility, longevity, and healthcare costs?

You are already on the right track!

Your decision to read 7 Steps to Financial Success is a brilliant first step. There are many books out there on retirement—some weighty tomes and some light as a feather. Some offer sound advice while others rely on age-old formulas and "truisms" that just don't hold up in today's complicated environment. I have read a lot of these and I can honestly tell you that Winter Troxel has succeeded where many others have failed. In under 100 pages, Winter has set forth a clear, straightforward, achievable plan for a sound retirement. In the process, has simplified the most complicated financial and retirement issues so that anyone can understand and act on them—including sequence of returns, maximizing Social Security, distribution planning, and retirement allocation. It is no wonder that he is fondly (and respectfully) referred to as the "Retirement Professor."

Trust me when I tell you that I have never come across a retirement book that offers so much useful information in such a concise, easy-to-understand, enjoyable context.

There is one great truth in the financial services industry that professionals hesitate to talk about: No financial advisor will ever care as much about your money as you do—no matter how much you pay him.

The Retirement Professor understands this inconvenient truth. His goal is to educate and empower you, so that you can participate actively in your own unique retirement strategy. It isn't about putting financial professionals out of business—it's about creating a partnership between you and your adviser.

At this point, you have two simple choices.

You can set this great book down, slowly back away, and continue on your current path—only to get blindsided by the next market collapse or financial emergency.

Or, you can turn the page and start absorbing the information you need in order make the best possible decisions about your retirement.

My heartfelt recommendation is this.

Turn the page.

• • •

As the co-founder of Ashton Strobelt, Abe Ashton is recognized as one of the top retirement consultants in the nation, helping thousands of individuals and families secure their retirements. Abe also serves as a nationally recognized mentor in the financial services industry.

Introduction

ccording to *US News and World Report*,[1] there are approximately 75 million baby boomers in the United States, and an estimated 10,000 people turning 65 every day. The trend is expected to continue for 20 years. This demographic shift out of the workforce and into retirement underscores the growing need for retirement education.

I started my career as a financial advisor over 12 years ago. During my first few years of working with clients, I came to realize that, within my profession, there was a disproportionate emphasis on growing wealth and a limited focus on the distribution of assets—regardless of the age or situation of the client. My training had been almost exclusively focused on planning toward retirement instead of planning for retirement, and that was the approach I took with my clients. I quickly came to understand the pitfalls of that approach, and began to rethink the way I did business. The purpose of this book is to let you in on the wisdom I've gleaned within my own practice, and to open your eyes to a new way of thinking about your retirement plans.

Michael Zwecher, professor of finance at Fordham University, estimates that fewer than 3 percent of financial advisors are "expert" in the discipline of distribution planning[2]. In other words, there are few professionals out there who are well equipped to help near-retirees and retirees navigate the unique challenges of using their assets to fund retirement.

It's a bigger problem than you might think. Planning for retirement has become a default exercise for most Americans: Individuals and families continue into their "golden years" employing the same plans and strategies they'd been following throughout their working years, in spite of the fact that the way they are using their assets is changing radically. During one's working years, it makes perfect sense to focus on saving and growing money. In retirement, however, the financial dynamic shifts toward using one's nest egg while endeavoring to sustain assets so as to avoid "running out."

A majority of the financial advice out there has an inherent bias. Investment advisors, who represent investment brokerage companies, tend to overly favor market-based strategies. Insurance agents, who represent life insurance companies, naturally favor insurance-based strategies. And then there's your "water cooler buddy" or successful uncle, who probably has an inherent bias toward what has worked within his own unique circumstances.

The objective of this book is to provide an introduction to effective distribution planning for near-retirees and retirees. Throughout the last decade, I've worked with hundreds of seniors unsure about their own preparedness for retirement and even less sure about how to "convert" their precious assets into income. The financial challenges of retirement can be overwhelming. It's my hope that this easy-to-follow, reassuring guide will dispel some of the fear and uncertainty that can accompany retirement planning, and replace them with the confidence and sense of well-being that come from having a solid, age-appropriate financial strategy.

In the chapters that follow, I outline the seven steps to building an individualized retirement income plan. The seven steps are:

1. Have a Master Plan for Retirement
2. Understand What is Essential to Your Quality of Life
3. Learn How to Maximize Your Fixed Income
4. Avoid Being "401(k) Poor"
5. Shift from an Accumulation Plan to a Distribution Plan
6. Determine Your Retirement Allocation
7. Select Your Strategy for Retirement Income

Retirees face a wide range of issues and it would be unrealistic to try to address all of them. My objective, rather, is to focus on the all-important concern of having ample resources to live comfortably and worry-free throughout retirement—whatever that might mean to you. When you close the cover, you should have a keener understanding of how you can use your retirement assets effectively, as well as a macro framework for your distribution plan.

My hope is that this book will spark an epiphany or two in your mind that will result in a life-changing adjustment to your financial life. You'll find some of my own experiences here, as well as those of my clients; a bit of humor; and some concrete solutions you can take to the bank. You won't regret taking an interest in your retirement future—and picking up this book is a good first step.

• • •

This seems like a good time to thank those who have helped me throughout the last decade, beginning with my wife, Corrie, who deserves a majority of the credit for my success. She has supported me from Day 1 and has provided a sounding board for my ideas for over twenty years. I also want to thank my sons, Braxton and Camden, for giving my life a steady dose of welcome imperfection. And—this may sound odd—I want to acknowledge all those in the industry who have provided examples of the wrong way to plan; they have pushed me to find higher ground for my own clients.

The challenges I've faced in my career have always inspired me to seek a higher level of understanding and subsequent business success. Many thanks to Michael Feeley, my business partner, for taking a leap of faith and joining our team. And finally, I need to mention my mother-in-law, Mary, for editing the very first draft of this book. It's amazing that I'm still in good standing with her, and I thank her for her patience.

1 Dave Bernard, "The Baby-boomer Number Game," *U.S. News and World Report*, March 23, 2012: www.money.usnews.com/money/blogs/on-retirement/2012/03/23/the-baby-boomer-number-game.
2 Michael Zwecher, *Retirement Portfolios: Theory, Construction, and Management, 1st Edition* (Wiley: January 26, 2010).

1

Step 1

HAVE A MASTER PLAN FOR RETIREMENT

I grew up in a small farm town in Indiana. Once every year or two, our family would go to the nearest amusement park for a weekend excursion. Cedar Point, in Sandusky, Ohio, featured all of the thrills any kid could imagine. I most vividly remember The Beast, the world's largest wooden roller coaster.

I was initially excited to ride this enormous coaster and eagerly joined the line of people waiting to get on. But as I stood there, I began to have second thoughts. I started to ponder the logic behind flying so high in the sky. Maybe it was a crazy thing to do. Maybe I'd be safer just staying on the ground. Of course, as a nine-year-old, I wanted to seem brave and grown up so I kept my fears to myself, secretly hoping I would be too short to be allowed on the ride. I just needed to be shorter than the Yogi Bear measuring stick at the front of the line. I knew it would be close.

As our family approached, my worst fears were realized. I was tall enough. That's when panic set in. We all got on the coaster and it slowly pulled away. I was wide-eyed and pale as the rickety little car slowly started climbing the first steep hill...click...click...click...click....

Looking back on the experience, I have to chuckle at my fear—though it was very real at the time. I was absolutely terrified of what would happen after the initial ascent. Would I be able to handle the twists and turns, the swoops and drops to come? Would I even survive the ride in one piece?

I'm sure you know I'm going to make an analogy between that childhood experience and the topic of this book—retirement—and here it is. Most near-retirees feel they should be excited at the prospect of their impending retirement after so many years of hard work. They should be eager to enjoy it, right? But a majority of the clients I work with initially express some reluctance or fear as they head toward "the front of the line." Like The Beast, retirement is uncharted territory, filled with unexpected twists and turns. It's my job to help alleviate the fear of what's coming and ease my clients into a successful and rewarding retirement. The first step toward that end is to have a master plan.

Client #1: No Plan

Dale had been working as a federal employee for over thirty years when I met him. He was planning to retire within the next year. As he finished up the last few months of his job, he wanted me to validate his plan.

Dale had never heard of "distribution planning" before we met. Instead he was mostly aware of the unknowns of retirement. He was worried about market volatility, inflation, and his own longevity. His anxiety over what might happen after he retired reminded me of my childhood fear as I stood in line for The Beast.

It's not that Dale hadn't prepared. Before I met with him, he had already evaluated his family's monthly expenses and tracked all of the pertinent numbers on a computer spreadsheet. He'd continually refined those numbers until he had squeezed out as many expenses as humanly possible. With what he believed was pinpoint accuracy, he had determined the least amount of money that he and his wife Rhonda would need for retirement.

The thing is...Dale's plan was really no plan at all. He was living in fear of the roller coaster known as retirement. Without a real distribution plan, he'd voluntarily stuck himself with an unnecessary pay cut in retirement. Dale and Rhonda had determined that they did not want to ride The Beast, preferring to stay on the ground where they would avoid the thrills and stay safe. Who can blame them? Their financial future hung in the balance.

What they didn't realize was that their alternative was equally terrifying. Dale and Rhonda were set to live out their entire retirement in fear and discomfort, as if in line for The Beast in perpetuity. Prevention mode, like anxiously awaiting a terrifying ride, can cause stress without end. How can you live a happy life if you are afraid to use your money? And what happens when the inevitable twists and turns do come along?

Dale had decided that the safest plan would be to downsize their living situation, continue to drive their old cars, and live on their fixed income throughout retirement, in spite of the fact that they had a net worth of over $1 million.

Common Rule of 4 Percent

For better or worse, most questions in life can be answered with a simple Internet query on Google. Whether the answer is the right one is another matter. If you don't have a retirement income plan and you don't know how to start constructing one, you might be tempted to Google around for the answer—and you'll find a number of them. I've learned from my many clients who started out by conducting such a search that the 4-percent rule seems to be the most popular answer out there—so let's look at it.

The 4-percent rule dictates that a retiree draw out four percent of his "nest egg" each year. So, for example, if you have $500,000 saved, your retirement income should be $20,000 per year.

The logic here is that, based on past market history, a 4-percent rate of withdrawal will sustain your assets over the course of your lifetime. In other words, it's a virtual guarantee that your money will last at least as long as you do.

A majority of retirement calculators available on the Internet use some variation of this rule—but you don't have to think too hard to come to the conclusion that following an elementary math formula does not constitute having a retirement income plan.

The problem with the 4-percent rule—well, one of the problems with it—is that it cannot prevent that anxious, roller-coaster feeling because it doesn't address the number-one retirement risk for most retirees: sequence-of-return risk.

Sequence-of-Return Risk

One of the main objectives of a retirement income plan is to plan for sequence-of-return risk, i.e, the inherent risk to one's income from the order of market returns. The biggest risk—and source of anxiety—for retirees is experiencing a down market at the "wrong time."

Near-retirees and retirees are most vulnerable to sequence-of-return risk in the period spanning the last five-to-seven years before retirement and the first five-to-seven years after it. The impact of a market downturn in these years can be life-changing for a retiree, much more so than for a younger person with more time to recover.

Sequence-of-Return Risk

Working 5-7 Years	Retired 5-7 Years
$250,000 Assets	7% Rate-of-Return Average 5% Withdrawals

Here's a hypothetical example illustrating the impact of sequence-of-return risk. In the example, the retiree takes 5 percent withdrawals, adjusted for inflation, from $250,000, over 30 years of retirement. During that period, the $250,000 grows at a 7 percent average rate of return.

Most people would assume that at the end of the 30 years, the retiree's total assets would be greater than they were at the beginning ($250,000) because the rate of growth (7 percent average) is higher than the rate of withdrawal (5 percent).

Let's take a look:

$250,000	5% Annual Withdrawals 3% Annual Increase	Hypothetical Annual Rate of Return	Positive Returns Early
65	$12,500	16.6%	$279,000
66	$12,875	7.4%	$286,771
67	$13,261	12.0%	$307,922
68	$13,659	11.3%	$329,058
69	$14,069	3.3%	$25,848
70	$14,491	20.7%	$378,740
71	$14,926	3.3%	$376,313
72	$15,373	8.8%	$394,055
73	$15,835	9.7%	$416,444
74	$16,310	14.3%	$459,686
75	$16,799	9.7%	$487,476
76	$17,303	7.2%	$505,272
77	$17,822	14.9%	$562,735
78	$18,357	9.1%	$595,588
79	$18,907	-3.2%	$557,621
80	$19,475	12.0%	$605,061
81	$20,475	8.1%	$634,013
82	$20,661	12.1%	$690,067
83	$21,280	11.9%	$750,905
84	$21,919	7.2%	$783,051
85	$22,576	6.7%	$812,939
86	$23,254	16.9%	$927,073
87	$23,951	7.1%	$968,943
88	$24,670	-3.0%	$915,205
89	$25,410	15.4%	$1,030,737
90	$26,172	8.3%	$1,090,116
91	$26,957	6.4%	$1,132,926
92	$27,766	-3.5%	$1,065,507
93	$28,599	-12.8%	$900,523
94	$29,457	-17.6%	$712,574

7%

You will notice that the retirement account balance is indeed higher. The $250,000 has grown to over $712,000!

What would happen if the exact same returns were received but the order of returns was different? What if the negative returns of the final three years in the table above happened in the first three years instead?

The average return would be the same: 7 percent. How much of the $250,000 would be left?

$250,000	
65	
66	
67	
68	
69	
70	
71	
72	
73	
74	
75	
76	
77	
78	
79	
80	
81	
82	
83	
84	
85	
86	
87	
88	
89	
90	
91	
92	
93	
94	

5% Annual Withdrawals 3% Annual Increase	Hypothetical Annual Rate of Return	Positive Returns Early	Hypothetical Annual Rate of Return
$12,500	16.6%	$279,000	-17.6%
$12,875	7.4%	$286,771	-12.8%
$13,261	12.0%	$307,922	-3.5%
$13,659	11.3%	$329,058	6.4%
$14,069	3.3%	$25,848	8.3%
$14,491	20.7%	$378,740	15.4%
$14,926	3.3%	$376,313	-3.0%
$15,373	8.8%	$394,055	7.1%
$15,835	9.7%	$416,444	16.9%
$16,310	14.3%	$459,686	6.7%
$16,799	9.7%	$487,476	7.2%
$17,303	7.2%	$505,272	11.9%
$17,822	14.9%	$562,735	12.1%
$18,357	9.1%	$595,588	8.1%
$18,907	-3.2%	$557,621	12.0%
$19,475	12.0%	$605,061	-3.2%
$20,475	8.1%	$634,013	9.1%
$20,661	12.1%	$690,067	14.9%
$21,280	11.9%	$750,905	7.2%
$21,919	7.2%	$783,051	9.7%
$22,576	6.7%	$812,939	14.3%
$23,254	16.9%	$927,073	9.7%
$23,951	7.1%	$968,943	8.8%
$24,670	-3.0%	$915,205	3.3%
$25,410	15.4%	$1,030,737	20.7%
$26,172	8.3%	$1,090,116	3.3%
$26,957	6.4%	$1,132,926	11.3%
$27,766	-3.5%	$1,065,507	12.0%
$28,599	-12.8%	$900,523	7.4%
$29,457	-17.6%	$712,574	16.6%
	7%		**7%**

The answer is none. So much for the foolproof 4-percent rule!

Because of sequence-of-return risk, a market downturn near the beginning of retirement can result in the complete failure of a retirement plan.

$250,000	5% Annual Withdrawals 3% Annual Increase
65	$12,500
66	$12,875
67	$13,261
68	$13,659
69	$14,069
70	$14,491
71	$14,926
72	$15,373
73	$15,835
74	$16,310
75	$16,799
76	$17,303
77	$17,822
78	$18,357
79	$18,907
80	$19,475
81	$20,475
82	$20,661
83	$21,280
84	$21,919
85	$22,576
86	$23,254
87	$23,951
88	$24,670
89	$25,410
90	$26,172
91	$26,957
92	$27,766
93	$28,599
94	$29,457

Hypothetical Annual Rate of Return	Positive Returns Early	Hypothetical Annual Rate of Return	Negative Returns Early
16.6%	$279,000	-17.6%	$193,500
7.4%	$286,771	-12.8%	$155,857
12.0%	$307,922	-3.5%	$137,141
11.3%	$329,058	6.4%	$132,259
3.3%	$25,848	8.3%	$129,167
20.7%	$378,740	15.4%	$134,568
3.3%	$376,313	-3.0%	$115,605
8.8%	$394,055	7.1%	$108,440
9.7%	$416,444	16.9%	$110,932
14.3%	$459,686	6.7%	$102,054
9.7%	$487,476	7.2%	$92,603
7.2%	$505,272	11.9%	$86,320
14.9%	$562,735	12.1%	$78,943
9.1%	$595,588	8.1%	$66,981
-3.2%	$557,621	12.0%	$56,111
12.0%	$605,061	-3.2%	$34,841
8.1%	$634,013	9.1%	$17,953
12.1%	$690,067	14.9%	($0)
11.9%	$750,905	7.2%	$0
7.2%	$783,051	9.7%	$0
6.7%	$812,939	14.3%	$0
16.9%	$927,073	9.7%	$0
7.1%	$968,943	8.8%	$0
-3.0%	$915,205	3.3%	$0
15.4%	$1,030,737	20.7%	$0
8.3%	$1,090,116	3.3%	$0
6.4%	$1,132,926	11.3%	$0
-3.5%	$1,065,507	12.0%	$0
-12.8%	$900,523	7.4%	$0
-17.6%	$712,574	16.6%	$0
7%	⟵⟶	**7%**	

The Solution:

Create a Retirement Income Plan

At some point during the slow climb up that first hill of The Beast, I realized that my pleas for help were useless; I might as well give in and enjoy the ride. And guess what? It was a blast! The first thing I wanted to do when I got off was get back in line and ride it again.

Retirement can be full of unexpected surprises—good and bad. Creating a retirement income plan can open up your financial life and point you toward a successful retirement without paralysis or a dependence on Internet calculators. It can protect you from the unknowns of the financial markets. A properly crafted retirement income plan will allow you to convert your accumulated assets into retirement income so you can sit back and enjoy the ride. The next chapter will discuss how to establish your retirement quality of life as the basis for a successful distribution plan.

Step 2

UNDERSTAND WHAT IS ESSENTIAL TO YOUR QUALITY OF LIFE

I was sitting watching television one evening when a commercial caught my attention. In it, a guy was standing on a ladder trimming the hedge around his suburban home. As he chatted with his next-door neighbor, a number floated over his head, representing how much money he would need to retire. Presumably, the investment company running the ad hoped that it would inspire viewers to call them and determine their own "magic numbers."

The ad prompted me to visit the company's website, where I found a calculator to help determine that all-important number. Out of curiosity, I went through the process—and I was not surprised by what I found. The company's calculations were based on the 4-percent rule—and the results were alarming! According to the website, I'd need quite a lot of money to retire comfortably.

A simple way to make a calculation based on the 4-percent rule is to multiply your near-retirement income by 25.

Near-retirement Income

$$\$100,000 \times 25 = \$2.5 \text{ million}$$

In other words, if you are making $100,000 at the end of your career, and you want to continue to live comfortably throughout your retirement, you'll need to have $2.5 million in assets. For most people, that's a pretty high hurdle.

Client #2: "I'll Never Be Able to Retire"

Suzanne was reluctant to meet with me. She was so timid and hesitant in our first meeting that I felt I'd imposed on her—but I wanted to help. After a conversation about non-financial matters, she mentioned that she felt she would never be able to retire. She should have saved more, she lamented—and then ticked off a list of all of her supposed transgressions regarding money. She actually *apologized* for her financial situation.

Whenever I run into someone like Suzanne—and believe me, there are a lot of Suzannes out there—I think about that "What's your number?" commercial and how it fuels people's insecurities about their financial lives. Suzanne was a perfect example of this; according to most predictors, including the one offered by the "What's your number?" people, Suzanne would need well over $2.5 million to retire comfortably—and she had "only" accumulated around $385,000.

She told me that the last financial advisor she'd met with said that she would have to work into her 70s or consider working part-time for the duration of her retirement. In fact, he'd felt her situation was so hopeless that he'd declined to work with her. No wonder she was reluctant to talk to me.

Her plan was to work forever.

I assured her she could do better than that.

Solution: Three Steps to Determining Your Essential Quality of Life

Step 1: Create a Retirement Budget the Easy Way

One of the most important aspects of near-retirement planning is understanding how much your retirement will cost—not what a boilerplate "magic formula" tells you, but the *true cost* of your retirement. The top-down approach is a simple way to estimate retirement expenses.

A. Start with your gross income

B. Subtract any payroll deductions (not including retirement account
    contributions)

C. Subtract your retirement account contributions

D. Subtract other regular savings

For example:

A.	Annual gross income:	$100,000
B.	Annual payroll deductions:	($ 30,000)
C.	Annual 401(k) contributions:	($ 15,000)
D.	Annual savings to investments:	($ 5,000)

Retirement budget estimate   **$ 50,000**

Step 2: Retirement Mindset

The next step requires that you take your mind off of the numbers and think
about the aspects of your life you consider essential. What's important to
you? What would you not want to live without? It's important to start getting
into a "retirement mindset" a few years before transitioning out of your
career. During the pre-retirement period, it's worthwhile to consider the
following factors:

- What are your most valuable social connections?

  Consider: family, friends, entertainment options, social opportunities, religious
  practice

- What will you do with your time in retirement?

  Consider: volunteer, travel, babysit, new career, hobbies

- What does your dream retirement look like?

  Consider: the quality of life you aspire to achieve and what that lifestyle will
  look like.

Personally, I love gathering up the daily newspaper from the driveway and
reading it during breakfast. That is something I never want to give up, at least

as long as newspapers are printed. My clients often discuss other retirement mindset preferences, such as spending time with grandchildren, traveling, hobbies, and where they desire to live.

Think about the above questions and discuss them with your loved ones. Remember, retirement is a great opportunity for a clean slate. You are no longer limited by school district boundaries or work commuting concerns. Your time is your own, to spend in ways that sustain and fulfill you. There are numerous choices to be made about what will enrich your quality of life in retirement and it's important to consider them carefully. This is the most exciting part of retirement planning–determining exactly what you want when you have no time restrictions and fewer responsibilities.

Take a moment to list the things you would not want to do without in retirement:

1. _____

2. _____

3. _____

4. _____

5. _____

Step 3: Make Retirement Adjustments

Now that you have spent some time envisioning your ideal retirement, it's time to adjust your Retirement Budget Estimate to reflect that vision–and make it a reality. What financial adjustments must you make in order to achieve the lifestyle you want in retirement? Notice, I haven't said you can have everything–but there may be some things you are quite willing to give up in order to have what is important to you. Do you really need that big home? Perhaps you'd consider downsizing so you can finance a vacation retreat or the exotic travel you've always dreamed of. On the other hand, if you intend to throw yourself into gardening or working in your wood shop, your house may be essential. This final step involves quantifying your new lifestyle to arrive at your *essential quality of life*.

Budget Estimate:	$50,000 (from Step 1)
Retirement Adjustments (expenses in retirement):	
Medicare:	$2,400
Travel:	$3,000
Second home:	$12,000
Hobbies:	$2,500
No more college bills:	$(10,000)
Total:	**$9,900**

Now we simply add the retirement budget estimate of $50,000 and the retirement adjustments of $9,900 to arrive at the cost of your essential quality of life.

Essential quality of life: **$59,900**

Essential quality of life is an after-tax number, so the last step is to convert the essential quality of life income estimate into a before-tax value. This is done by dividing your essential quality of life number by the difference between 100 percent and your effective tax rate.

Before tax adjustment:

Essential Quality of Life divided by (100% minus Tax%)

$59,900/(100%-25%) = $79,866

The before-tax adjustment accounts for the taxes that will be paid once money is received as income from retirement accounts. In other words, in the above example, the retiree's essential quality of life costs $59,900. But, since taxes have to be paid on income, he would actually need $79,856 per year in order to net that $59,900. The rest would be paid out in taxes.

**Income needed (before taxes)
to fund Essential Quality of Life:**   **$79,866**

Your own gross number—the real amount you'll need—can be derived by
dividing your essential quality of life number by the difference between
100 percent and your assumed tax percentage. (In the above example, it's
25 percent).

• • •

You may have noticed that the income needed to fund the essential quality
of life in the above example is more than $20,000 lower than the working
income. For most, the actual income needed in retirement is lower than your
working income before retirement. After calculating your current quality of
life cost and making retirement adjustments, you arrive at your *retirement
essential quality of life*.

It's important to note that your retirement adjustments are meant to
account for positive or negative changes to cash flow from before and after
retirement. For example, Medicare will be a new expense in retirement while
not paying tuition will increase cash flow.

So...what's your number?

If you believe the television commercials or Internet calculators, then
$100,000 of working income requires having $2.5 million in assets by
retirement—for many, an impossible dream. But when you evaluate replacing
your income from the perspective of net or take-home income, the payroll
deductions that will not apply to your retirement—such as Social Security and
contributions to your 401(k)—are accounted for, so you get a more realistic
view. You'll find it is a much more encouraging one.

In the next chapter we discuss how to figure fixed-income assets such
as Social Security into the equation, too. Are you starting to see that your
number may be more reachable than you thought?

Client #2: " I'll Never Have Enough" Revisited

Once I walked Suzanne through the steps I've outlined above, and she developed a more realistic picture of the income she would need to fund her essential quality of life, she was astonished. She'd only need $66,000 per year in retirement income to replace her working income of $108,000! She made me run the numbers three times before she believed me. After considering her Social Security and federal government pension, she realized that she could comfortably retire on her assets of $300,000.

Step 3
LEARN HOW TO MAXIMIZE YOUR FIXED INCOME

A few years ago, my wife and I decided to go on a family trip to Myrtle Beach. We thought it would be a good place to visit because it was far enough south to find decent weather but close enough to drive to from Washington, D.C. The only thing I was worried about was a stretch of I-95 immediately south of DC that I refer to as "hell." This section of the Interstate, stretching down to Fredericksburg, Virginia, seems to be backed all day long. It's unbearable. I do whatever I can to avoid it.

But there's no way around it if you want to go to Myrtle Beach—so I came up with a plan. I pulled my kids out of school a day before spring break started and we headed out of town on a Thursday night around 9:00 pm. My plan was to get past Fredericksburg before 11:00, stop for the night, then enjoy a clear path to our destination the next morning. Perfect.

We left the house on time—a minor miracle in itself—and soon got to that reviled portion of the Interstate. It was smooth sailing for the first mile, but just as I was congratulating myself for my cleverness, I spotted brake lights ahead. After 30 minutes of stop-and-start traffic I started to get irritated; at one hour, I wanted to curl into a ball; and at two hours, I was convinced we'd have had a more relaxing spring break at home. Finally, after a three-hour crawl, we passed a construction truck setting out cones for an overnight project. All the planning in the world could not have helped me avoid this particular problem because it's impossible to predict road conditions with any real accuracy. There are just too many variables.

I think about that experience every time one of my clients asks me, "What is the best age to start collecting Social Security benefits?" Although timing can be important, it isn't the only variable. Decisions about Social Security must be based on the individual situation.

The question seems simple enough—and of course the payment amounts at age 62, full retirement age, and 70 are listed on the second page of every Social Security statement. But the decision bears some thought, and clearly, my clients understand this. When attempting to answer the question for yourself, I want you to consider the following hypothetical situation.

Triplets and When to Take Your Benefit

Imagine three identical brothers, triplets who mirrored one another throughout their lives in every imaginable way. It was their objective to remain in identical positions financially, too. The brothers bought similar homes, took out similar mortgages, worked for the same employer for the same salary, and contributed the same amount to their 401(k)s. At retirement, there were no measureable financial differences between them.

Then a difference arose. The brothers decided to start drawing their Social Security benefits at different times.

Earl decided to start his benefits at age 62.

Stan decided to start his benefits at age 66.

Del decided to start his benefits at age 70.

Which brother ended up receiving the most money from Social Security?

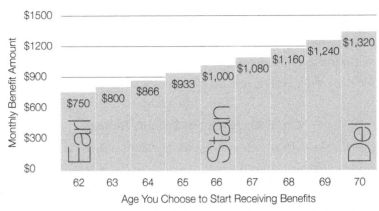

This hypothetical example assumes that each triplet earned the same amount of Social-Security-eligible income in past years.

So, who made the best choice? As you might have guessed, the determining factor is mortality.

Total Social Security Income Received

	Earl	Stan	Del
Age	62	66	70
Monthly Benefit	$750	$1,000	$1,320
Income at 70	**$74,988**	$48,993	$0
75	**$124,994**	$113,054	$81,246
80	$177,563	**$180,398**	$166,657
85	$232,825	$251,194	**$256,444**
90	$290,920	$325,618	**$350,833**

Figures include a 1 percent cost-of-living adjustment (COLA).

As the above table indicates, Earl initially received the most income; at a certain point, Stan overtook him; and ultimately, Del came out on top. That's assuming that all three brothers lived into their 80s.

As you consider the above example, it's important to note that your financial circumstances are unique to you. In the *real* world, there are no three people with identical financial lives. As a result, your approach toward your fixed-income assets should be unique to you and your own financial situation.

The problem most retirees create for themselves concerning Social Security is that they do not make decisions about their benefits in coordination with their other retirement assets. For some reason, most think about their Social Security benefits in isolation from their 401(k), IRA, and pension.

Client #3: No Social Security Strategy

I met Charles and Susan a couple of years ago. Charles was a federal employee and had requested a retirement consultation after participating in one of my firm's retirement workshops. When we met, the couple was about six months from retirement. They were waiting until they turned 66—Susan in June and Charles in August. Charles wanted a second set of eyes on his plan for retirement just to make sure he hadn't left anything out.

Here's an overview of their plan: Charles and Susan had several retirement accounts to go along with their federal pensions and Social Security. He had determined that they would receive approximately $134,000 per year from their main retirement accounts (his TSP and her 401[k]) and fixed income.

Charles and Susan's Plan for Retirement

Fixed Income Assets

Owner	Asset Type	Age at Retirement	Annual Income
Charles	Federal Pension	66	$40,000
Charles	Social Security	66	$30,000
Susan	Social Security	66	$18,000

Retirement Accounts

Owner	Asset Type	Amount of $	Annual Income
Charles	TSP	$850,000	$34,000
Susan	401(k)	$300,000	$12,000
Susan	IRA	$18,000	
Susan	Old 401(k)	$39,750	
Susan	IRA	$27,500	
Susan	Old 403(b)	$69,000	
Susan	IRA	$39,850	
Total		$1,344,100	$134,000

Charles and Susan intended to start drawing their Social Security benefits at age 66 and they felt very confident about their overall plan. Yet, they were lacking a *true* strategy for Social Security.

Missing Benefits

At first glance, most of the plan seemed sound; $134,000 of income would be enough for them to enjoy quality of life beyond their working years. But I concluded that they were going to leave money on the table. In other words, their lack of a Social Security strategy would result in fewer benefits.

As I started to evaluate the specifics, I noticed that they did not have a plan for Susan's assortment of retirement accounts. These accounts were relatively small individually, but together equaled over $194,000. The seed for a Social Security strategy was born.

Here were the factors I considered in recommending a deferment—and thus, an upgrade—in their Social Security income:

1. Charles and Susan's Social Security benefits would be $17,000 higher per year if they deferred taking their benefit another four years.

2. Susan had multiple IRAs and retirement accounts from different jobs over the years that totaled over $190,000 but were not a part of their overall plan.

Considering these two facts, I advised them to defer their Social Security benefits to age 70. By doing so, their benefits would increase by $17,000! To replace the lost income during the deferral period, I recommended drawing from Susan's "forgotten" retirement accounts.

Susan's Retirement Savings $194,100

Social Security Income Replacement for 4 Years

$48,000 Per Year

Charles and Susan's New Plan—with Social Security Strategy
Fixed Income Assets

Owner	Asset Type	Age at Retirement	Annual Income
Charles	Federal Pension	66	$40,000
Charles	Social Security	66	Deferred
Susan	Social Security	66	Deferred

Retirement Accounts

Owner	Asset Type	Amount of $	Annual Income
Charles	TSP	$850,000	$34,000
Susan	401k	$300,000	$12,000
Susan	IRA	$194,100	$48,000
Total		$1,344,100	$134,000

In the table above, you will notice that the income generated from Susan's consolidated retirement accounts replaces the $48,000 in Social Security benefits they would have drawn between ages 66 and 70.

After the four-year deferral period, the consolidated IRA would be exhausted—but Charles and Susan would be 70 and could then apply for their maximum Social Security benefit. In the table below, you can see that their Social Security income would increase by $17,000 per year. Not bad, considering that their benefit base will adjust for inflation for the rest of their lives.

Charles and Susan's Plan with Social Security Strategy at Age 70
Fixed Income Assets

Owner	Asset Type	Age at Retirement	Annual Income
Charles	Federal Pension	66	$40,000
Charles	Social Security	66	$39,500
Susan	Social Security	66	$25,500

Retirement Accounts

Owner	Asset Type	Amount of $	Annual Income
Charles	TSP	$850,000	$34,000
Susan	401k	$300,000	$12,000
Susan	IRA	$0	$0
Total		$1,344,100	$151,000

Lost Opportunity Cost

During the distribution period, retirees are always making decisions with lost opportunity cost implications, and Social Security is no different. Is it better to take more from your 401(k) early and defer Social Security—or to take Social Security as soon as possible? The objective of a retirement income plan should be to minimize the lost opportunity cost when taking income from assets. That's so important I am going to repeat it. *The objective of a retirement income plan should be to minimize the lost opportunity cost when taking income from assets.*

Coordinating your Social Security benefits with your other assets is the best way to ensure that you are getting the most out of your financial situation.

Big Picture and Pensions

In the overall planning picture, fixed-income assets such as Social Security and pensions lay the income floor for most retirees. It's imperative to leverage those assets and get the most out of them. Doing so reduces the pressure on defined-contribution assets (IRAs, 401[k]s, TSPs) to produce income, and the result is more financial flexibility in the long term. Fixed-income assets, such as Social Security, serve as a foundational piece of retirement income, so it's crucial to maximize your benefits.

MATCH THE USE AND PURPOSE OF YOUR MONEY

One of the most important shifts at retirement time is to consider the purpose of the assets you have accumulated throughout your lifetime. Will you be using them for your children's or grandchildren's college tuition? For your own retirement income? To buy a beach house? Travel?

My friend Jerry lives in Cincinnati, Ohio. He's approaching retirement age, and every time goes on vacation, he falls in love with the place. When he came back from a week in Hawaii, for example, he told me excitedly, "I'm going to quit my job, find my purpose in life, and move to Maui!"

I wasn't too surprised that he found Maui more desirable than Cincinnati. It's got perfect temperatures, beautiful surroundings, and great food. And for the week Jerry spent there, he had nothing to do but enjoy it all. But, as a friend, I felt compelled to be the voice of reason. I mean...Jerry couldn't really quit his job at that point. He still had to make a living—and, was he really ready to leave his friends and family behind? Even if he waited until retirement and his wife was on board with his plan, would a radical move make him happy in the long run?

Knowing Jerry, I figured that in the final analysis, he would stay in Cincinnati rather than picking up stakes for Maui, Las Vegas, Miami, New York, or any of the other places that had captivated him. At heart, he knew where he belonged, understood his own comfort zone, and would continue to build upon the successful financial and emotional life he'd created. Even if he could move, and enjoyed contemplating the possibility, he'd choose not to.

In retirement, it's important to figure out what you really want to accomplish and how you can use your assets to achieve those goals—and it is crucial that you be realistic about that. Moving to Maui might sound good, but perhaps a condo on the local golf course, among friends, will make you happier in the long run. These decisions can be quite daunting.

If you're more than 10 years away from retirement, then you want to create as much flexibility as possible because the future—including the time between now and retirement—is more uncertain. If you're closer to retirement, then you want to start tailoring your accounts to your retirement mindset.

Your ultimate goal should be to correctly match the purpose for your money with the accounts and investment strategies best designed for that purpose.

Examples of Connecting Purpose to the Type of Account

Use for Money	Type of Account
Bills	Checking
Emergency	Savings
Retirement Income	Retirement Accounts (401[k], TSP, IRAs…)
Second House	Regular Investments or Savings
Travel	Regular Investments or Savings

Everyone must find his or her own "perfect balance," taking into account the need for retirement income as well as any planned expenditures that might fall above and beyond the basic budget.

Avoid Becoming 401(k) Poor

In my experience, a majority of human resource directors, water-cooler experts, and financial publications encourage employee participation in employer-sponsored retirement accounts such as 401(k)s. Rodney Brooks of *USA Today* advises, "If you're 50 or older, take advantage of the 'catch-up' provision, which lets you put additional money into your plan each year" on top of the annual maximum.[3] I've often encountered clients who admit limited financial literacy, but still espouse the benefits of their 401(k). I could write an entire book on how a majority of Americans, who cannot agree on anything politically, seem to be 100 percent behind their retirement account at work. Instead, I'll just spend a little time discussing the implications of putting too much money into these types of accounts—which include a whole alphabet soup of names such as 403(b), 457, SEP, and TSP.

Client #4: I Have No Money for College

I met Carl and Diane a few years ago and I still remember our first few moments together. They walked into my office with their heads down and Diane appeared to be on the verge of tears. As we shook hands, Carl stared directly through me. What was going on? I assumed they were stressed over a financial disaster or overwhelmed by debt.

To my surprise, neither of those things was true. Carl and Diane had over $800,000 in their retirement accounts and no debt. They had secure jobs and were making good incomes. I couldn't figure out why they were so distressed until Diane said, "The reason we came to see you is because we have to write a check for $20,000 for our oldest son's college tuition and we don't have the money."

My clients were 401(k) poor. In other words, although they were on track to have over $1 million at retirement, they didn't have access to even $20,000 of it for an important expenditure right now. All they had was about $5,000 in their savings account. Everything else went toward covering their basic expenses.

"I thought we were doing everything the right way," Diane continued. "We've always contributed the maximum to our retirement accounts, as everyone advised us to do."

As you get closer to retirement, it's important to recognize the need for different types of assets and to think about the limitations and benefits of the 401(k). The goal is to avoid becoming 401(k) poor during the period when you might need money from savings, while still assuring you'll have sufficient money for retirement.

No Fun Tax Zone: It Counts as Income

My partner, Michael Feeley, does not ordinarily buy lottery tickets, but a few years ago the Mega Millions jackpot got so big he couldn't resist the temptation to get one. I decided to get one, too. That evening, on my way home, I started to daydream about what I would do if I actually won $300 million. It's amazing how quickly I managed to burn through millions of dollars in my imagination!

What if you won the lottery? What would you do with the winnings?

For the purpose of this chapter, let's say you are the lucky winner of a million dollars—but there's one catch. The money will go directly into a tax-deferred retirement account such as a 401(k) or TSP. Let's assume that this money is extra—above and beyond the retirement accounts you currently have.

Now, let's have some fun. Let's buy a beach house. We have a million dollars to spend, so let's put $500,000 of it into a lovely little cottage by the ocean.

You probably know the first thing that happens when you withdraw the $500,000 from the deferred retirement account: It is taxed. This is the part most retirees understand. The retirement accounts they amassed while working are taxable in retirement.

What you might not understand—what many retirees fail to take into account—is the second, and more damaging, tax consequence associated with the transaction. The withdrawal increases your income, in the eyes of the IRS, by an extra $500,000!!!

In other words, the purchase of the beach house with your lottery winnings increases your income by $500,000, rocketing you into a new, considerably higher tax bracket—which will then be applied retroactively to ALL of your income for the year. Here's a breakdown:

	Regular Year	Year with Beach House Purchase
Regular Income:	$70,000	$70,000
Extra Withdrawal:	$0	$500,000
Tax Rate %:	15%	39.6%
Taxes on Regular Income:	$10,500	$27,720
Taxes for Beach House:	$0	$198,000
Total Taxes:	$10,500	**$225,720**

The beach house purchase increases the amount of taxes you'll have to pay for the year by over $215,000! In other words, you will only net $285,000 from the $500,000 withdrawal.

I realize I set up a loaded example here to make my point. In real life, it is unlikely that you would use money from a 401(k) to buy a beach house or to subsidize any other large purchases. Certainly not if you are tax averse. But the implications of this example are important. I want you to understand, first and foremost, that tax-deferred accounts were designed to be used for retirement income only. The government penalizes large withdrawals from them and rewards smaller withdrawals over time.

Everyone's Doing It, Then Reality Hits

It's difficult to sit across the table from retirees who realize that they do not have the flexibility they need because of overfunding their IRAs and 401(k)s while working.

Throughout our working years, we are surrounded by voices telling us to save as much as possible in our 401(k)s, to maximize our IRAs—so it's no surprise that a majority of our clients come to us with a disproportionate amount saved into these accounts. The wise course of action would have been to determine how they planned to use the money they were accumulating up until retirement, so they could buy into the most effective assets for their purpose. It is never too late to make adjustments, even in the years immediately preceding and just after the start of retirement.

3.   Rodney Brooks, "8 Tips to Maximize Your 401k for Retirement," *USA Today*, October 7, 2014: www.usatoday.com/story/money/columnist/brooks

Step 5
CREATE A DISTRIBUTION PLAN

Peer pressure can be amazingly powerful. To this day, I regret never figuring out how to roll up my jeans in the same "cool" way that Johnny Johnson did—but you can be sure I tried! Peer pressure has caused many of us to value the wrong things or make bad decisions over the years. Like it or not, our sense of self worth is based at least in part on the external validation of others.

What if "peer pressure" concerning the proper way to handle your money in retirement comes from the financial industry? Can you see how that pressure might lead to a multitude of bad decisions? I believe that pressure from "accumulation" advisors—as well as from co-workers—leaves a majority of retirees stuck in the distribution period (i.e., retirement) with an old accumulation plan.

What's your favorite sports team to root for? Mine is the Florida State University football team. Let's imagine a scenario where Florida State is beating its rival, the University of Florida, by three touchdowns at half time. I can see myself cheering, tweeting my friends, and feeling excited about the game. Then, unaccountably, University of Florida comes roaring back in the second half and wins the game.

Would I go in to work the next day and say, "Yes! Florida State won the first half!"

Of course not. At the end of the day, it is only the final score that matters.

Financially, retirement isn't the end of the game. Retirement is "half time."

The period before retirement, *the accumulation period*, involves saving and growing your money for the future. That's the first half of the game.

The period after retirement, *the distribution period*, is when you spend the money you saved, which replaces the income you earned during the accumulation period. The distribution period is the second half of the game— and the time when the final score comes in.

I want all of our clients to be ahead at half time, just as my beloved Florida State was in that football game. But I recognize that they have to win the second half of the game, too–the distribution period.

Client #5: Do You Like my Accumulation Plan?

Judy and I first met about nine months before her planned retirement. She had been working with an accumulation planner for over 20 years and she was excited to show me his plan for her retirement. Mainly, she was enthused by its conclusion: She would have a secure retirement.

I was surprised that Judy wanted to meet with me, but she explained that she was looking for a "rubber stamp": someone to validate her plan and say, "Job well done."

As I looked over the details, I was pleasantly surprised to see that her income objectives were appropriately met. I skipped ahead in the report, past all of the green graphs and pie charts, to the disclosure page. That's where a particular statement caught my attention: "Your retirement projections are based on a portfolio return of 6.139 percent per year for the 35 years of your plan."

In the last 35 years, do you know how many times the S&P 500, an indicator of US market performance, has made 6.139 percent? None. Some years, the rate of return is higher than others; and some years it is substantially below zero. What about sequence-of-return risk (Step 1)? Clearly, it hadn't been accounted for.

Moving on, I noticed that in Judy's plan, all of her assets were pooled together for income withdrawals. As a result, her income would be permanently impacted by financial emergencies.

I left my rubber stamp in the drawer.

If she pursued the course of action her advisor had mapped out for her, Judy would be stuck in an accumulation plan throughout her distribution period.

The Problem

The economics of money change over the course of your lifetime. Your money operates one way when you are saving it, during your career, and another way when you start to make withdrawals in retirement. During your working years, the timing of market ups and downs has no impact on the money you will have at the end.

Here is a table illustrating four years of variable returns and the corresponding monetary outcome.

Return Order #1

Year	Beginning Balance	Rate of Return	Ending Balance
1	$100,000	23%	$123,000
2	$123,000	18%	$145,140
3	$145,140	-7%	$134,980
4	$134,980	-18%	$110,683
Average		4%	
Actual		2.5%	

Here is a table illustrating four years of the same variable returns and the corresponding monetary outcome when the order of the returns is different. You can see that the outcome is the same.

Return Order #2

Year	Beginning Balance	Rate of Return	Ending Balance
1	$100,000	-18%	$82,000
2	$82,000	-7%	$76,260
3	$76,260	18%	$89,986
4	$89,986	23%	$110,683
Average		4%	
Actual		2.5%	

Conclusion? During the accumulation years, the order of market returns has little impact on the future value of the account.

Actual Rate of Return versus Average Rate of Return

As a brief aside, it is worth noting the difference between actual return and average return in the above example. In both instances, the average rate of return is 4 percent but the actual (based on monetary balance) is 2.57 percent. The cost of volatility, in this case 1.43 percent, is rarely taken into consideration when an accumulation plan is employed during the distribution period.

The Problem

The problem for retirees is the difference in how money grows in retirement— and this problem is compounded by accumulation planners who use linear math to project future financial success. In Diane's case, her advisor wants to keep her in the very same investments in retirement that she's been in during her working years, assuming that the market will yield a linear return for 35 consecutive years! The plan completely ignores the realities of market fluctuation.

It's absolutely critical to understand that *accumulation strategies do not work during the distribution period.*

Let's look at the same returns we mapped out above, but add annual withdrawals of $4,000 at the beginning of each year.

Return Order 1 with Withdrawals

Year	Beginning Balance	Withdrawals	Rate of Return	Ending Balance
1	$100,000	$(4,000)	23%	$118,080
2	$118,080	$(4,000)	18%	$134,614
3	$134,614	$(4,000)	-7%	$121,471
4	$121,471	$(4,000)	-18%	$96,326
Average			4%	
Actual			3.1%	

Here is a look at the second set of numbers with these withdrawals:

Return Order 2 with Withdrawals

Year	Beginning Balance	Withdrawals	Rate of Return	Ending Balance
1	$100,000	$(4,000)	-18%	$78,720
2	$78,720	$(4,000)	-7%	$69,489
3	$69,489	$(4,000)	18%	$77,277
4	$77,277	$(4,000)	23%	$90,131
Average			4%	
Actual			1.6%	

When withdrawals are added into the equation, the order of returns changes the outcome after four years, in spite of yielding the same average return. In the Order 1 scenario, the average rate of return is 4 percent and the monetary outcome is $96,326. In the Order 2 scenario, the average rate of return is 4 percent and the monetary outcome is $90,131! In accumulation planning, the only way to correctly predict the outcome of a withdrawal strategy is to be able to predict the exact order and rate of return for each and every year of retirement. Obviously, that isn't possible.

The comparison above looked at only four years. Imagine how variable the results would be if we were to evaluate multiple decades (see page 19). In retirement, the further we look into the future, the more vast the potential outcomes become – even as our ability to predict those outcomes decreases.

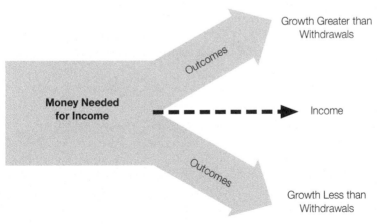

Growth Greater than Withdrawals

Money Needed for Income

Income

Growth Less than Withdrawals

Accumulation Plan versus Retirement Plan

After a recent federal government workshop, an attendee asked me, "How do I know if I have an accumulation planner rather than a distribution planner?" Here are the most common signs that you continue to pursue an accumulation plan when what you need is a retirement plan:

- Does your plan use the 4-percent rule?
- Does your plan rely on an assumed return throughout retirement?
- Does your plan protect against sequence-of-return risk?
- Does your plan include income assets and discretionary assets?
- Does your plan factor in your Social Security benefit and other income-producing assets?

Winning the Game, Not Just the Half

To "win" at retirement—i.e., to insure that you will have enough money to meet your personal retirement goals—you must be able to convert your assets for use in retirement. This involves leaving growth strategies in the past and focusing on your desired outcomes during the distribution period. How much income do you need to live as you wish? What amount of money should be available for travel and emergencies? Is your plan protected from sequence-of-return risk? A successful retirement necessitates leaving the accumulation period behind and implementing a distribution plan based on a new allocation.

Distribution planning starts with identifying the purpose for your assets. In other words, what will you use your money for in retirement?

- Household expenses
- Vacations
- Large purchases (i.e. cars, home projects, second homes)
- Income replacement
- Pass on to beneficiaries

List the types of expenses you expect to incur in retirement:

_____

_____

_____

_____

_____

_____

_____

_____

Now, it's important to identify what types of assets would best fund your desired uses. We learned earlier that retirement accounts are not appropriate for large expenses because of taxes.

Here is a brief list of the most common types of assets and the ways they are most often used as part of a well-designed distribution plan.

- Savings/Checking Accounts   liquidity, emergencies, discretionary spending
- Non-Qualified Investments   growth and discretionary spending
- Retirement Accounts   income replacement
- Annuities   income replacement
- Life Insurance   pass on to beneficiaries and estate planning
- Pensions   income replacement

Armed with a better understanding of what constitutes a sound distribution plan, it's time for the next step: developing a new retirement allocation!

Step 6
CREATE A RETIREMENT ALLOCATION

I signed up for my first investment account in my first year out of college. I had very little understanding of the choices out there, so I had no clue what to select. I finally picked one mutual fund from each asset risk class and ended up with a colorful pie chart on my statements. I later learned that these somewhat arbitrary choices formed what was known as my "asset allocation."

I don't think my process was that unusual. From what I've seen, most novice savers select their asset allocations without really understanding how an appropriate mix of investments can impact their retirement. (And realistically, how much thought are we giving our retirement at age 22 or even 30?)

As we move into our peak earning years, many of us enlist the help of financial advisors to review and adjust our asset allocations–and these professionals are more than eager to help. Financial planners employ a variety of methods for determining the best way to allocate savings–and later, a safe withdrawal strategy for retirement income. But the balancing act between portfolio management and income planning can be quite daunting when considering the unknowns of retirement.

Although accumulation planners have successfully developed methods for determining their clients' optimal asset allocation, they are less successful at–or even focused on–distribution planning.

The Problem

Understandably, most near-retirees are comfortable with the approach to money they have taken throughout their entire working life. They have been savers for so long that it's difficult to figure out how to actually *use* their nest egg. If it weren't for the fact that the IRS has instituted Required Minimum Distributions to "force" withdrawals from retirement accounts, some savers might remain downright paralyzed—unwilling or unable to touch their own carefully accumulated wealth at the appropriate time!

Here's another story meant to help illustrate my point.

Every Saturday morning my dad used to come into my room and announce, "Your list of chores is on the kitchen counter." I'd lie in bed for a while longer, dreading the thought of those chores. Then I'd drag myself down to the kitchen where I would dawdle through breakfast and watch *Alvin and the Chipmunks*.

Eventually, I'd work my way through the dreaded list. The whole time I was working, I'd think about how unfair my life was. None of my friends had to endure similar misery. Why, oh why, did I have such mean parents? Why was I forced to clean my room and mow the grass? If it were up to me, I wouldn't have bothered. By the time I was done, it was 2:00 or 3:00 in the afternoon; the best part of the day was gone!

Clearly, my parents knew that sometimes we have to be forced to do what's best for us. Which brings us to Required Minimum Distributions. Why do they exist? Probably, because most retirees lack the will and understanding to properly use their retirement monies. Most are untrained as to how to use their money. If it weren't for RMDs, they might put off drawing out any money at all—which would have a severe impact on their essential quality of life.

Getting back to my "rotten childhood," one Saturday I had an epiphany. When Dad woke me up, I quickly popped out of bed, wolfed down my breakfast, and headed outside. I was going to be proactive and finish my chores as quickly as possible. I knew they'd only take two hours if I worked efficiently, and then I'd have most of the day to play with friends or watch baseball on TV. Bingo. I'd figured out how to obey my parents' rules *and* have a great weekend.

In retirement, the objective is to pick an efficient and appropriate income strategy early on, one that will ensure a good quality of life as well as a secure future. A proactive distribution allocation will lead you down the path to that end.

Thousands of new retirees who have saved their whole lives to provide for their later years hesitate to reward themselves with a quality of life aligned with their net worth. They are racked with uncertainty over the unknowns of market volatility and longevity: Saving money is easier than spending it when you feel as if you are staring into the darkness of an unknown future.

Transition Toward Retirement

In an ideal plan, the transition between the accumulation period and distribution period occurs over the last 5-10 years before retirement. During this time, the financial approach shifts from an accumulation emphasis on *growth* to a distribution emphasis on *growth and income*.

The set of graphs below show a two-step transition from the accumulation phase to the distribution phase. During the first step, the near-retiree shifts his assets from equities (stocks and mutual funds), bonds, and cash to equities, income-oriented assets, and cash. This first move is designed to maintain a similar level of overall risk in the asset allocation while beginning to build protection around the money that will be needed for retirement income. It involves converting one's conservative holdings (i.e., bonds, CDs, money market) into income-oriented assets.

Transition from Accumulation Allocation to Retirement Allocation

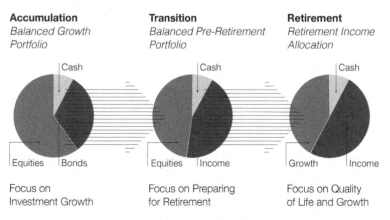

Accumulation	Transition	Retirement
Balanced Growth Portfolio	Balanced Pre-Retirement Portfolio	Retirement Income Allocation

Cash — Cash — Cash

Equities | Bonds — Equities | Income — Growth | Income

Focus on Investment Growth — Focus on Preparing for Retirement — Focus on Quality of Life and Growth

The second step, which comes during the last few years before retirement, is to align income holdings with essential quality of life (see Step 2) and to finalize the retirement allocation.

Retirement Allocation

The purpose of the new asset allocation strategy we recommend for retirement is to balance the use of assets for *essential* and *nonessential* uses. This approach involves coordinating retirement assets with expenses for retirement. After determining your essential quality of life, you segregate a majority of your assets into two categories.

On the one hand, the floor of your allocation is made up of both fixed assets (i.e., Social Security and pensions) and conservative, income-oriented vehicles. The objective here is to maximize income from a specified pool of resources and minimize the exposure to market loss.

On the other hand, the nonessential is put into market-based investments. With the safety provided by the floor, the overall retirement picture is less vulnerable to market volatility. Discretionary monies can be invested in the market without fear of disrupting the quality of life provided by the floor assets. A snapshot of this strategy looks like a pyramid.

Retirement Allocation Pyramid

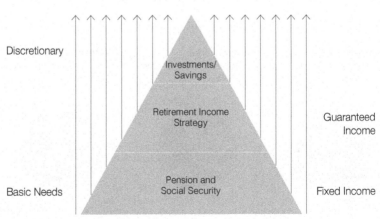

Client #6: Creating a New Allocation

John recently came into the office to meet with Michael and me. He spent the first 20 minutes of our meeting sharing all of his positive experiences with his current financial advisor. Over the years, he said, his advisor had been honest and seemingly aligned with John's goals and objectives.

Considering his good relationship with his advisor, I was curious as to why he was meeting with us—so I asked him what he hoped to accomplish in our time together.

"I need a distribution plan," he said, "and although my advisor is good at growing my money, I think I need someone new to show me how to *use* it."

How wise of John to realize this, I thought, *when so many people don't.* We proceeded to walk him through the steps outlined so far in this book.

We talked about the importance of having a retirement income plan (Step 1).

We worked together to determine his essential quality-of-life costs. (Step 2).

We selected a strategy for his Social Security (Step 3).

At that point, we were ready to create a retirement allocation.

His income from fixed assets (Social Security and pension) was projected to be approximately $30,000 per year.

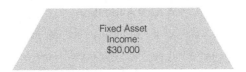

Based on John's Essential Quality of Life, his optimal retirement income came out to $60,000.

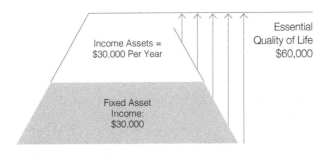

John's asset position included $700,000 in various investments. After determining his fixed income (Social Security) and his essential quality of life, we knew how to allocate that $700,000 of total assets. First, I recommended that he segregate those assets into two categories: *essential* and *non-essential* (or discretionary).

Essential = assets designated to fund retirement income up to essential quality of life.
Discretionary = flexible assets above and beyond essential quality of life.

Based on John's income need of $30,000 (the difference between his essential quality of life and fixed-asset income), we recommended that he allocate his $700,000 as follows:

$500,000 Income

$200,000 Discretionary

By following that formula, John can safeguard his desired quality of life throughout his retirement (via his income assets), while maintaining the necessary flexibility for unexpected events (via his discretionary funds).

A New Allocation

Imagine a retirement where all of your income needs are met without the fear of running out of money. And, any time "the world" requires expenditures above your budget, you can use another "bucket" of money to meet those needs. This vision of retirement is attainable. All you need is a new allocation.

Step 7
DETERMINE THE APPROPRIATE INCOME STRATEGY

A fter determining your retirement allocation, your next step is to figure out the most appropriate income strategy for your situation and preferences. In other words, what is the best way to draw out the money you've dedicated to income? Choosing an income strategy is one of the most critical steps toward building a plan for a successful retirement; yet, there is no "one-size-fits-all" approach that addresses everyone's needs. In some instances, multiple income strategies may even be desired.

You must've anticipated that I'd have a story for you here.

During the last several months, I have been evaluating companies and options to replace the windows in our home. When I started, I had no idea what I was getting myself into. The first guy who came out to the house to provide a "free estimate" took measurements, discussed his company's product, and told me the bottom line would be $30,000. I was flabbergasted. That much? I didn't say anything and within 30 seconds he asked how I would feel about $20,000. Holy cow, the price of windows dropped by 30 percent in 30 seconds, just because I was momentarily speechless. I decided to not talk at all, and by the time he was done, the price of windows had dropped to around $15,000.

There were two problems with his presentation. First, I felt suspicious of the drop in price. What if I'd agreed right away and paid twice as much as necessary? Are there some people out there gullible enough to pay $30,000 for a $15,000 job? Add that to the fact that I'd never heard of the window company before I saw their ad online, and this guy was out of the running. I didn't buy the windows and I basically had to push him out of the house.

The second guy I met with was more creative. He, too, started at around $30,000, then dropped to $20,000–but then he didn't budge. When I told him that the price was too high, he said, "Okay, well how about this idea? We just started working in the Philadelphia market and we sold a ton of windows, but some of the customers turned out to have bad credit and couldn't pay. I may be able to get some of those unused windows for you at special price." He made the call and, sure enough, it was my lucky day! I could get the Philadelphia windows for just $13,000.

No thanks. The whole thing seemed shady to me (forgive the pun) and I checked this guy off my list as well.

The same kind of thing can happen when working with a financial planner. Products get promoted that prove lucrative for the adviser but might not fit well into your comprehensive distribution plan. In my experience, fewer than 1 in 10 retirees have a real distribution plan!

Before getting into the options, it's important to remember why having an income strategy is so important.

Avoid Running Out of Money

Your number-one risk during distribution is longevity. That means just what you think it does: You do not want to run out of money while you are living. You may not be accustomed to thinking about longevity as a "risk"–but in the context of your finances, it most certainly is–and all retirement planning must include consideration of it. Let's look at an example.

If you have $500,000, is it advisable to withdraw $100,000 per year? If you do so, how long will your money last? Five years? Six? With such aggressive withdrawals, it certainly will not last for the duration of a 20-to-30-year retirement.

The purpose of a retirement income strategy is to determine how to maximize your income while protecting you against longevity risk.

Sequence-of-Return Risk

Sequence-of-return risk also poses a significant threat to a successful retirement. As we discussed earlier, sequence-of-return risk is the negative impact of negative market returns during the five years before and after retirement. A double negative—where the market loses at the same time that a withdrawal is taken—is the Kryptonite of any income strategy in retirement: the one thing that can bring you to your knees, financially speaking. During the accumulation years, investors typically recover from market losses, but the dynamic changes when you are taking money out of your accounts rather than saving. Here's an example.

Income Assets:	$500,000
Desired Income:	$20,000

	Market Return	Amount	Income	Withdrawal Rate	Balance
Year 1:	4%	$500,000	- $20,000	4%	$500,000
Year 2:	-40%	$500,000	-$20,000		$360,000
Year 3:	??	$330,000	????		???

The impact of the 40-percent market loss in Year 2 drastically compromises the retirement assets that will be needed for another two to three decades. Does a 40-percent loss seem like a farfetched exaggeration? It isn't. I assure you that the impact of a market correction during the distribution phase can be devastating. How much income can you safely take from a balance of $360,000? Presumably, it would not be prudent to continue withdrawing $20,000 per year for income.

Armed with an understanding of the problems, let's consider the retirement income strategies designed to offset them.

The 4-percent Rule

In 1994, William Bengen, an MIT graduate, developed the 4-percent rule, which states that a withdrawal of 4 percent of retirement assets per year is probably safe—meaning that the retiree will not run out of money in his lifetime. (This assumes that he is invested in a market mix of stocks and bonds.)[4]

For example, if you have $500,000 invested, you could safely withdraw $20,000 per year, or 4 percent of the total.

Positives of this approach:

- Simple to understand and implement
- Most common; probably what your friends are doing

Negatives of this approach:

- No protection from sequence-of-return risk
- Minimum amount of income per dollar accumulated
- No longevity protection

Most accumulation planners utilize some form of the 4-percent rule. "Sophisticated" advisors use computer simulation software to refine the rule and market portfolio, making the process a bit more scientific, while others stick with a simple, linear percentage. No matter the method, the positives and negatives remain.

Laddered Withdrawals

One primary objective of distribution planners is to reduce the sequence-of-return risk for clients. The withdrawal ladder approach seeks to reduce this risk by allocating income assets into multiple "buckets" designed to be used over the course of retirement. For this purpose, retirement is divided into phases.

Ladder Withdrawal Approach

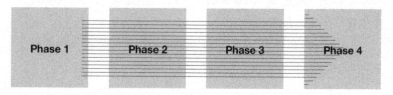

The investment plan for the first two buckets, which contain funds meant to be used during the first two phases of retirement, is more conservative, so as to avoid sequence-of-return risk. The money in the final two buckets is invested for growth because it will not be needed for several years.

For example, if you have $500,000, first you must divide it into multiple buckets representing your four retirement phases. Each phase typically lasts between 5 and 7 years, depending on your age at retirement. The first bucket is completely full at retirement, and each subsequent bucket has less money in it initially. The first bucket is used for income during the first phase, and so on. While one bucket is being used for income, the others are growing. In total, most withdrawal ladders aim for a 6-percent withdrawal rate for retirees. In other words, $500,000 of assets will provide approximately $30,000 per year in retirement income.

Positives of this approach:

- More income than when following the 4-percent rule (6 versus 4 percent)
- Sequence-of-return risk is accounted for

Negatives of this approach:

- Longevity risk (there is no money after the last bucket is consumed)
- No guarantee that the last buckets will be able to replace funds withdrawn from the initial buckets

Deferred Annuity Approach

There are many types of annuities available to retirees, and they offer an array of benefits. There are so many options, in fact, that I believe the real purpose of these instruments has been lost on the general public. Annuities were created for income. At the same time, annuities are complex and often come with limitations on liquidity during the initial years.

In the beginning, annuities involved a trade with an insurance company: The retiree literally traded his retirement assets to the insurance company in exchange for lifetime income. Who got the better deal? That depended strictly on the mortality of the retiree. These types of annuities still exist in the form of Social Security and defined-benefit pension plans, but individuals rarely purchase these "immediate annuities" anymore.

Over the last couple of decades, the most common choice of annuity for retirees has been the deferred annuity. As its name implies, this annuity involves a deposit of funds, a deferral period, and then the commencement of withdrawals for income.

Using this approach, you put your retirement assets into a deferred annuity in anticipation of withdrawing money during retirement. The deferred annuity should include an income rider to protect your retirement income. The deferred annuity approach involves a fee (in the range of .75-1.25 percent) to have your income protected for life. In other words, you are paying to make sure that if your retirement assets were to run out, the insurance company would subsidize your income. Properly set up, a deferred annuity also allows your retirement assets to grow even as you are withdrawing them during retirement.

Deferred Annuity

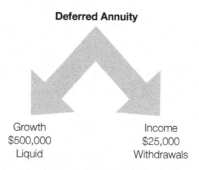

Growth
$500,000
Liquid

Income
$25,000
Withdrawals

For example, if you retire with $500,000 and have a 5 percent income benefit, your income will be $25,000 per year—guaranteed—for the rest of your life. You will have your $500,000 and can take withdrawals from it. The balance of your assets will still enjoy market-based growth during the withdrawal period: If growth outpaces withdrawals, your account balance will go up. If growth lags behind withdrawal, your account balance will down. Your surviving beneficiaries will receive the remaining balance.

Positives of this approach:

- Better Income than 4-percent rule (5 percent+ versus 4 percent)

- No sequence-of-return risk

- No longevity risk

- Ability to pass on assets to beneficiaries

Negatives of this approach:

- Less growth potential than most mutual funds

- Most deferred annuities do not offer full liquidity without a fee for the initial years

- Wide range of fees across companies and types (from very low to very high)

Buffering Approach

In this strategy, the retiree sets aside two years of income in a safe account, such as a money market or savings account, and keeps the rest in his retirement portfolio. In years when the market portfolio underperforms, income can be drawn from the safe account, thus preventing double negatives. In years when the market portfolio exceeds the withdrawal rate, the safe account can be replenished. This approach looks like this:

$20,000 income

$460,000 retirement portfolio

$40,000 safe account

The buffer-zone strategy reduces the risk of double negatives and provides an opportunity to increase income over time if your portfolio balance exceeds where it started.

Positives of this approach:

- Mitigates against double negatives

- Opportunity for increased income over time

- Maximum flexibility

Negatives of this approach:

- Usually involves market risk
- Lower income than ladder or annuity approach

Custom Strategy for You

At this point, you must be wondering which of these approaches we recommend to our clients—and to you. The answer isn't that simple; it doesn't necessarily involve choosing one approach and sticking with it. Often, we recommend a custom approach that involves an allocation across strategies. There are no rules. We recommend building an approach that fits your unique situation.

Okay, you're thinking, but what strategy do you offer most frequently? Although I don't keep official statistics on the matter, the most common strategy involves a combination of investments (4-percent rule/Buffer Strategy/Ladder) and annuities (deferred annuity strategy). We find that the best strategy balances opportunities for growth and certainty of income.

A custom strategy takes into account your essential quality of life, asset composition, investment tolerance, and retirement preferences. Ultimately, you want to find the right balance among income risk, amount of income, and the ability to realize your essential quality of life throughout your retirement. A well-informed retirement planner can help you make these determinations and craft the right plan.

When choosing a retirement planner, it is imperative that he or she be fluent in the array of withdrawal strategies available—and not simply an expert in one approach alone. Now that you have a basic understanding of the various approaches, you are better equipped to find the right advisor, and to take an active role in your own retirement planning.

4. William P. Bengen, "Determining Withdrawal Rates Using Historical Data," *Journal of Financial Planning*, October 1994: 14–24.

Conclusion
HOW TO PLAN FOR YOUR RETIREMENT

Life lessons come from the most unexpected places, and inevitably come at times when we're not even in the mood to be taught. That said, I have a feeling that you picked up this book at exactly the right time, and have persisted in completing it because you sense how important its lessons are to your immediate and long-term future.

Building a financial foundation for retirement isn't easy. When you're in your 30s, your financial priorities are weighted toward buying your first house, subsidizing your growing family, and establishing yourself. When you're in your 40s, you spend time and money on your kids' activities, home improvements, and upgrading your quality of life. In your 50s, the reality of retirement starts to set in—and panic can follow, as you start to evaluate how much you'll need in order to retire comfortably. All along the way, life throws its own curves, including health concerns, market fluctuations, family needs, and career adjustments.

So...how do you begin thinking about retirement? You want to be able to turn to a financial services professional to guide you, but it can't be just anyone. Even the trusted financial adviser who has been taking care of your money for decades may not have the right answers. If you take away just one thing from this book, I hope it is that not all financial advice is equal—and much of it is ill-suited to the needs of those facing retirement.

Sadly, over the last decade, very few of the clients who have walked through my door are equipped with a sound distribution plan for retirement. Most of them are still saddled with an accumulation approach at a time when they desperately need to shift gears and adopt a distribution approach. That's where I come in—and that's why I wrote this book.

It's my hope that the basics I've outlined here can help you avoid the pitfalls of pursuing the wrong approach to retirement—and allow you to enjoy your retirement to the fullest, free of the financial uncertainty. But keep in mind that they are just that—basics. I have purposely kept this book simple, to provide you with an overview of the options you face and the pros and cons of each possible approach to retirement distribution. I could have written an entire book about each approach—but that's where your financial adviser comes in. At the very least, you now know the right questions to ask—and that is half the battle.

Although many of the tools I describe in these pages can be used without the help of a financial adviser, I highly recommend that you team up with a good distribution planner near the beginning of your retirement. You've worked hard for your money and now you're facing the best time in life—the time to enjoy the fruits of your labors. Armed with the basic knowledge I've provided here and the assistance of a savvy and committed financial professional, I know you can make a smooth transition into a rewarding retirement.

Publisher's Note

This book provides general information that is intended, but not guaranteed, to be correct and up-to-date. The information presented is not presented as a source of investment, tax, or legal advice. If you need investment, tax, or legal advice please consult with a competent financial advisor, accountant, or attorney to address your situation.

The contents of this book should not be taken as financial advice, or as an offer to buy or sell any securities, fund, type of fund, or other financial instruments. The information presented is not to be considered investment advice. The reader should consult a registered investment advisor or registered dealer prior to making any investment decisions.

The author does not assume any responsibility for actions or non-actions taken by people who have read this book, and no one shall be entitled to a claim for detrimental reliance based upon any information provided or expressed herein. Your use of any information provided does not constitute any type of contractual relationship between yourself and the provider(s) of this information. The author hereby disclaims all responsibility and liability for all use of any information provided in this book.